AWKWARD
FAMILY
PET PHOTOS

AWKWARD
FAMILY
PET PHOTOS

MIKE BENDER &
DOUG CHERNACK

BANTAM PRESS

LONDON · TORONTO · SYDNEY · AUCKLAND · JOHANNESBURG

TRANSWORLD PUBLISHERS
61–63 Uxbridge Road, London W5 5SA
A Random House Group Company
www.transworldbooks.co.uk

First published in the United States
in 2011 by Three Rivers Press,
an imprint of the Crown Publishing Group,
a division of Random House, Inc., New York

First published in Great Britain
in 2011 by Bantam Press
an imprint of Transworld Publishers

A CIP catalogue record for this book
is available from the British Library.

ISBN 9780593069349

Addresses for Random House Group Ltd companies outside the UK
can be found at: www.randomhouse.co.uk
The Random House Group Ltd Reg. No. 954009

Printed and bound in China by Toppan Leefung

Book design by Maria Elias
Cover design by Daniel Rembert
Cover photo submitted by Nathan

4 6 8 10 9 7 5 3

This book is dedicated to our pets.
Thank you for not judging.

Contents

Introduction

There are few things more rewarding than having a pet. They love us uncon-
ditionally, shower us with attention, and they actually help us live longer.
So, what can possibly be awkward about our animal BFFs? Well . . .
nothing. In truth, *we're* the awkward ones. We adore our pets and treat them like
members of the family, but let's face it—sometimes L-O-V-E makes us go a little
overboard. Like giving them elaborate names, throwing them birthday parties, and
making them a Christmas sweater to match with the rest of the family. As proud
animal owners ourselves (a dog named Din-Din and a fish named Porky), we too often
forget that what these gentle creatures cherish the most is our companionship. This
book celebrates our well-intentioned but sometimes misguided affection and shines a
light on the wonderfully awkward side of pet ownership.

When we launched AwkwardFamilyPhotos.com in May 2009, the pet photos
quickly became our most popular and most commented upon pics. So, in June 2010,
we dedicated a separate site to that special connection between people and their pets
and called it AwkwardFamilyPetPhotos.com. And soon enough, strange pictures came
pouring in from all over the world, and they weren't just of cats and dogs. They also
included birds, bunnies, chickens, goats, monkeys, frogs, snakes, raccoons, skunks,
and, quite frankly, some animals we never even knew existed.

Beyond what can be found on the website, this book also features exclusive never-before-seen photos, "behind the awkwardness" stories, and peculiar tales from a veterinarian. To capture the authenticity of each kind of pet owner, we also invited guest contributors to open each chapter by writing about their own experiences. What struck us was that whether they had a dog, cat, or monkey, the devotion between human and animal was the same.

We want to thank all of the amazing families who were self-deprecating enough to send in their pet photos. Without them and their sense of humor, none of this would be possible. And of course we want to thank our pets. We know we do things that are perplexing, but they never hold it against us. They are our role models, our little Buddhas, and our sense of calm in a tumultuous world. Perhaps their most loving gesture of all is allowing us to be awkward. And for that, we are very grateful.

Mike Bender and Doug Chernack

AwkwardFamilyPhotos.com
AwkwardFamilyPetPhotos.com

1

The Pet Portrait

O ur pets will go along with anything to make us happy and there is no greater symbol of that than the pet portrait. This is the opportunity to capture our animals the way we think they look best, pictured by our side or on their own. So we do their hair, dress them in fancy outfits, plot out their stiff poses, and ask them to "smile" as they stare into a flashing light. Sure, they probably think the whole thing is ridiculous, but they never complain. And while our pets may never ask us for doubles, these photographic gestures are our way of letting them know that they are much more than just our animals . . . they're family.

NORTHERN EXPOSURE

Winston thought his natural coat should have been sufficient.

TOP MODEL

Don't hate this opossum for being beautiful.

THE PHODOGRAPHER

Kirby is more comfortable behind the camera.

CATSCAN

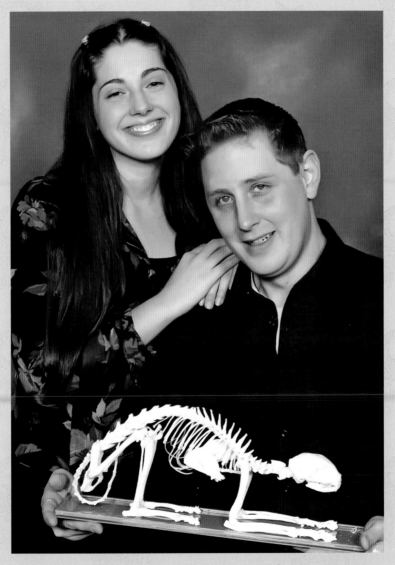

It's never too late to capture that perfect moment.

READY FOR MY CLOSE-UP

We want them to look perfect for the camera. Something tells us they don't always share our enthusiasm.

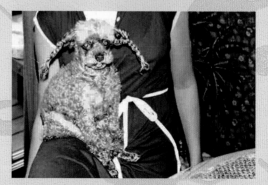

BORN IDENTITY

Max wasn't convinced of his Dutch descent.

THE NEW GUY

The cat was really hoping things wouldn't work out.

PETPOURRI

There are "cat people," "dog people," "bird people," and then there are "animal people." Here's to those families who believe variety is the spice of life.

FIELD TRIP

It felt good to get off the farm.

DOPPELGÄNGERS

For some animal lovers,
a portrait of their pet just
isn't enough.

FIREHOUSE DOG

The Dalmatian tried to warn them that the concept was contrived.

HANDLE WITH CARE

Because there's nothing a skunk loves more than being touched.

PET NOIR

Some mysteries will never be solved.

BEHIND THE AWKWARDNESS

Please note that these rabbits didn't all actually like each other, but they did all live in the house with us. This photo could not have been possible without the fourteen bunny-wranglers and gigantic quantity of Cheerios (some of which you can see on the floor by the rabbits). We also had three cats and three rats living with us at the same time.

The Hyde Family
Houston, Texas

This was in 1987. I was sixteen years old and had the
fabulous idea for my sister, Kim (who was fourteen), and
I to dress alike and put matching bows around our new
kitten's neck. Our kitten was a boy, named Sam.

Angie
Edmond, Oklahoma

29

Our family would always bring pets to the Olan Mills photo studio. We brought all our dogs, chickens, even a potbellied pig once. This time, we each showed up with a pillowcase containing a snake. After this picture, we weren't allowed to bring any more animals.

The Smith Family
Woodland, California

This is a photo of my husband, me, and our dog, Scooter. Poor Scooter. About six weeks after this photo shoot, we adopted our baby daughter and his life changed forever!

Becky
The Woodlands, Texas

ONCE UPON A DOG

Proof that generations of pets have looked into the camera and wondered, "WTF?"

2

Dogs

Some dogs own the couch. Some dogs own the bed. My dog, Millie, owns the house. Her name isn't on the title or anything, but she is absolutely certain that it is her house and that I simply live there as well. I've had a dog psychic come over and tell her that it is in fact *my* house and *I'm* the mommy—but it's no use. Sure, she waits for me by the door, wags her little tail, and snuggles with me when we're watching TV, but make no mistake, she's the alpha female and I am her humble slave. She didn't come by this opinion randomly—friends point out that she owns more outfits than I do, has more toys than I do, and even has more hairstyles than I do.

I would do anything for Millie. I have defied surly flight attendants to let her sleep on my lap during flights. I once came close to killing a coyote with my bare hands simply because he dared to stand outside my house and make Millie whimper. And yes, she has a special gown to wear on Oscar night and for *The Bachelor* finales. Does that make me strange? Maybe, but that also makes me the lucky girl who gets to live in Millie's house.

Karen
Los Angeles, California

DOGPILE

When you have a pile named after you, you expect to be on top.

SWITCH

Houston hoped this would bolster his case for table scraps.

CLOSE ENCOUNTERS

If Cody had a treat for every time he was abducted . . .

NEW KID IN TOWN

For Maggie Moo, four is a crowd.

DON'T YOU FORGET ABOUT ME

They're the center of attention and then without warning, someone else crawls onto the scene. Can we blame them for wanting to stay in the spotlight a little longer?

38

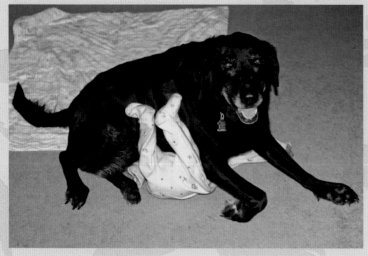

PROM DATE

A yes is a yes.

BENJAMIN BUTTON

One of these toddlers is actually forty-five years old.

YOU RAISE ME UP

This owner attempts to take the friendship to new heights.

THE SOUND OF SILENCE

Rowley had stepped outside for a little peace and quiet.

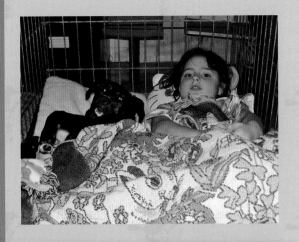

CAGEY

We give them their own spaces so they can learn to be comfortable by themselves . . . but dogs aren't the only ones who suffer from separation anxiety.

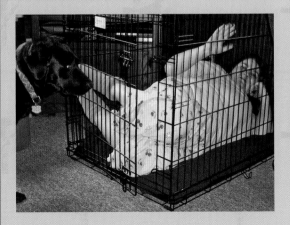

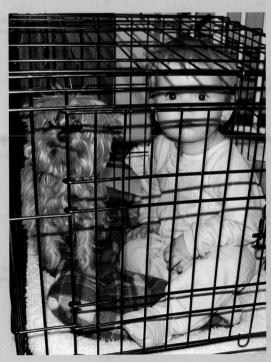

FOILED

Shiloh was waiting for a little help from above.

TALES FROM A VET: THE PRINCESS DIARIES

The names have been changed to protect the awkward.

Her name was Mrs. Shaeffer. She was a very wealthy woman whose husband had passed away and left her a fortune. My staff would talk about her black American Express card and how she seemed to have a different car every month. I was only exposed to her in the exam rooms, but each time, she was a sight to behold. She had a small Pomeranian named Princess, and they were like twins. When Mrs. Shaeffer wore her Prada cream-colored coat and Louis Vuitton shoes, Princess had the exact same matching outfit. The detail was incredible, even down to the diamond collar. I tried to be as professional as possible with her, but one day I had to ask about the outfits. Mrs. Shaeffer said that she had a tailor for Princess who made her clothes and shoes. She also had a dresser who helped Princess make outfit changes throughout the day. And it wasn't just Princess—Mrs. Shaeffer had done this for each of the eight dogs she owned. I said that it must have been hard to make clothes for all of them. Mrs. Shaeffer told me that the hardest part was finding a designer that the dogs approved of.

AFPP SPECIAL RECOGNITION

There's a reason we call them man's best friend. They're loyal to a fault and never complain. However, there are some dogs who go above and beyond the call of duty and for that, AFPP would like to bestow its highest honor to the one and only Chessey.

STOGIE

Snuffy swears that he has never inhaled.

PALER SHADE OF BROWN

This family decided to color coordinate.

DOUBLE-D

Meet his pride and joy.

INSEPARABLE

There *is* such a thing as too much love.

PET-A-LIKES

There is a theory that people look like their pets. We now have the evidence.

OPPOSITES ATTRACT

And they said a friendship like ours could never last.

He was always flaunting his six-pack.

OFF

Children are not allowed on the furniture.

AWKWARD DOG NAME

MR. BRIAN BUBBLEGUMS

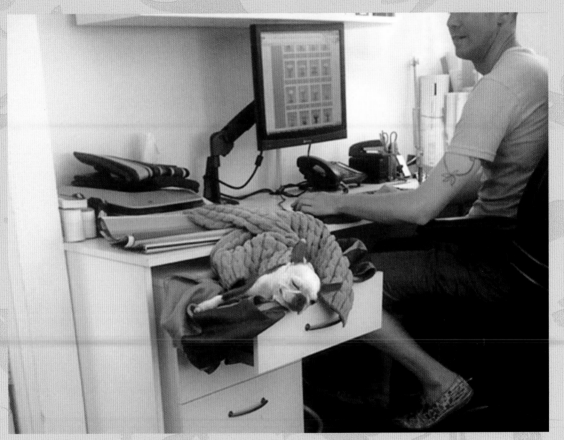

It was "Bring Your Pet to Nap Day."

REFLECTIONS

Loby and her owner were experiencing an existential crisis.

BUNCH OF BALLOONEY

Little Bruno wasn't as happy with his designer shoes.

BEHIND THE AWKWARDNESS

I'm the awkward little girl in the front. The wolf was borrowed from the Bell Museum of Natural History, and my mom thought it would make a nice subject for a Christmas card. Our dog, Dynamite, was terrified.

Kelly
Ramsey, Minnesota

For my mom's birthday, we decided to use her church picture (yes, she took the dog with her) and put it on a T-shirt. Note the uncanny similarity between our dog Velcro's hairstyle and my mom's.

Carrie
Royal Oak, Michigan

After entertaining my daughter for about three hours, my mother was running out of ideas. Apparently, desperate times call for desperate measures and Tinker, the dog, was the victim of such measures. My mom chose to dress up the poor dog in old baby clothes and put her in a stroller. While my daughter was thoroughly entertained, Tinker wasn't so sure.

Jillayne
Haddon Township, New Jersey

3

Cats

Like any mother, I love my kids. I revel in their achievements, I scold them when they're bad, and I commiserate with other moms over feeding, health, and behavior issues. I carry their photos in my wallet, ready to whip out and display proudly to anyone who asks about my family. Casual acquaintances are bemused (and sometimes confused) to discover that my "kids" are in fact three cats, although they may already have deduced this from the patina of cat hair on my clothing.

Many people with human children just don't get it. But I know that my furry family fulfills me in an incalculable way and satisfies my maternal instincts. I may not change diapers, but I change the litter box and while I don't wake up in the middle of the night to a crying baby, I have woken to a meowing one. I would not leave a burning building or evacuate my home until I was certain that all of the cats had gotten out safely. If destitute, I would go hungry to ensure the cats had enough to eat.

While those who don't understand might call me a "crazy cat lady," I think the real "crazy" ones are those who don't open their hearts and homes to all deserving souls.

Karen
Castro Valley, CA

SLUMP

The only thing Howard promised was that he would show up.

BRIDESMAIDS

He always thought her friends were a little catty.

WARM AND FUZZY

A reminder that cuddling is a privilege, not a right.

THE STARTER KIT

She had some growing up to do before she was ready for
one of her own.

CAT GUYS

We're all familiar with "cat ladies," but AFPP is proud to recognize their lesser-known but equally as passionate male counterparts.

SLEEPOVER

Normally, Possum doesn't allow her owner to sleep in the bed.

CENTER OF ATTENTION

Larry agreed to share the spotlight as long as everyone else agreed to stay out of it.

BEHIND THE AWKWARDNESS

Believe it or not, it wasn't even Halloween—this was my everyday wear. My brother used to be mortified and would yell, "Mom, Alex is acting like a cat again!"

Alex
Victorville, California

We won a portrait session in a raffle for the holidays and since all our friends were taking photos with their families, we decided to take one with our kids! It was quite an undertaking, considering neither of them liked to be held. At one point, Fudgie got loose and we had to corner her. The sad part is, I don't recall feeling it was an odd thing to do.

Terry
Bellmore, New York

The instructions from the photographer were to "let your personality shine with one of your favorite mementos." Not much of an athlete in high school, and with no major scholastic awards or achievements to my name, I opted for Patches. Unfortunately, she was not as enthusiastic, leaving behind several mementos of the scatological persuasion in one of the choir practice rooms. The girl with the horse-riding equipment really had to clear out of there in a hurry.

Jake
New Haven, Connecticut

When I was a child I was absolutely obsessed with cats, particularly this cat, who I named Wormser because he had a nasty case of ringworm when we adopted him (that was an itchy summer). I forced that cat to sleep with me, suffered multiple scratches as he attempted to escape my clutches, and ordered a subscription to *Cat Fancy* to keep abreast of all things Russian Blue.

Gillian
Chicago, Illinois

AWKWARD CAT NAME

LADY SCHRODINGER UNDERFOOT DE VELCRO

UNEVEN STEVENS

She was starting to doubt that it was an equal trade.

THE MISTOFFELEES

This family poses with their outdoor set of cats.

TALES FROM A VET: HAIRBALLS

I keep a bottle of Benadryl on my desk at all times because I have terrible allergies to cats. And when I'm around a cat owner, they usually flare up—that is, except when I'm around Mrs. Jones. She cares very genuinely for her numerous Persian, Himalayan, and other long-haired breeds, all of which she has rescued. I've been to her house on several occasions, and you must be thinking that I reach for the bottle of Benadryl before I go over there, but the house is immaculate and I am always surprised at the lack of cat hair on the furniture and floor.

I had received a sweater vest from Mrs. Jones as a present and one day when I was scheduled to visit, I decided to wear it to show my appreciation. Unfortunately, there was not enough medicine on the West Coast to help me with my allergies that day. In fact, I had to be rushed to the hospital because of a severe reaction. When the doctor asked me if I had been exposed to anything new, the only thing I could think of was the vest. I called Mrs. Jones to apologize for missing our appointment and explained that I had to go to the hospital. I also asked her what the vest had been made of. She proudly told me that it came from 100 percent Jones family cat-hair balls.

THE PUSSYCAT DOLLS

You can't join the group until you're ready to cat-ccesorize.

PUBLIC TRANSPORTATION

This kitten would rather walk.

SQUEEZE PLAY

When we're kids, we just want to hug and kiss everything that is cute and cuddly . . . only problem is, these kitties aren't stuffed with cotton. We can report that no felines were harmed in the awkwardness.

4

Birds

When I left home at eighteen, I had to leave my beloved dog Wilma behind. I knew I wanted another pet, but after everything I had just been through with Wilma, it had to be something easy to take care of and that I wouldn't get too attached to. A friend suggested a cockatiel, saying that they were intelligent, and that I'd never become as attached to a bird. I was sold.

I entered a local pet store and asked an employee if they had any cockatiels. She returned a few moments later with a shoebox. Inside was the most hideous, featherless, pathetic-looking bird I'd ever seen. The employee explained that because the bird was so fragile, it would need constant care and attention. I turned to the employee and said, "I'll take it." I don't know why, but seeing that defenseless little creature just melted my heart.

When I brought the bird home, I noticed that it was constantly bobbing its head. Thus, I named my new best friend Bobby. From then on, we were inseparable. Looking back, I realize my friend was wrong about the connection between me and my bird, and I couldn't be happier about that.

Jennifer
Hibbing, Minnesota

STARING CONTEST

Little Jake had never met a bird he couldn't intimidate.

CHICK MAGNET

She had a thing for cocky guys.

CATCHING SOME DDD'S

86

For some, it's a warm glass of milk. For others, it's a duck on the head.

BIRDBRAIN

It might not be the most comfortable perch, but at least we know they're always looking out for us.

NESTING

You should see how they respond to the Three Wolf Moon T-shirt.

BIRDS OF A FEATHER

The duck thought he wore it better.

HANGTIME

It was the only way she could get the rooster to talk.

BEHIND THE AWKWARDNESS

It was late at night and my Sun Conure was sleeping in his fuzzy hut as usual. I thought it would be cute to get a shot of him, but quickly realized when you flash a bright light into a birdcage in the middle of the night, it's downright terrifying.

Kathy
Cincinnati, Ohio

That's me when I was eight years old visiting my grandmother in Oklahoma. That summer a pigeon flew into her yard, and from that moment it never left our side. It went everywhere with us—riding in the pickup to go grocery shopping, visiting the salon, and, of course, to the portrait studio for a classic glamour shot.

Loren
Chicago, Illinois

WINGMEN

They're strong, sexy, and tender enough to handle one of nature's most delicate creatures. There's no squawk about it—a man and his feathered friend are a one-two punch nobody can resist.

5

Farm Animals

W hile most of the kids I grew up with had cats or dogs, my family lived on a farm full of chickens, pigs, and goats. Now, I know there is a perception that farm animals are more livestock than they are pets, but if you've ever lived on a farm, you would know that's not true. Just like cats and dogs, we played with our pets, taught them tricks, talked to them, took them on walks, and nursed them back to health when they were ill. Of all of our animals, we were closest to our goats. Each one earned a name and a rightful place in our family like Daisy, Bluey, Jack, Cali, and good old Nubie. For competitions in fairs, my sister would create pageantlike themes and dress herself and the goat in matching outfits (my mother may be one of the few people in the world who knows how to sew a Batman outfit for a fully grown goat).

Our goats were such a big part of my childhood that it was a tradition to take photos with them and hang the portrait in the living room. Some of my classmates might have thought this was a little odd, but we liked to think it was a fitting tribute to our beloved friends.

Erica
Athens, Ohio

HORSEFRONT RIDING

Horseback is so last season.

THE HAM

There always has to be a camera hog.

PET-A-LIKES

BALLS OUT

This is why they chose the birds and the bees.

THERE'S A HORSE IN THE LIVING ROOM

There's a horse in the living room.

ASS-KISSER

It wasn't the first time Megan had been caught brown-nosing.

VESTED INTEREST

Becky was starting to regret her choice of outfit.

WALKING THE GOAT

This goat was suffering from two identity crises at once.

WILD HORSES

A gentle reminder that we want the photographs; they don't.

PIGS IN A BLANKET

At first glance, they might not look like the most cuddly animals, but these lap hogs love to snuggle.

BEHIND THE AWKWARDNESS

While Shuffy and I are "striking a pose," my aunt seems to have contracted some sort of disease causing her to turn into a zombie who craves moderately priced fashion items.

Paige
Alvaton, Kentucky

This picture was taken after my dad bought himself a 4H steer at our county fair. He was so proud that he made my whole family pose with it, including my poor mother, who was very pregnant at the time. The best part is that my dad had this photo blown up to 11 x 16 and prominently displayed it on our living-room wall for years and years.

Camie
Riverton, Wyoming

If it weren't for "vigilant" mothering and "dutiful" sistering, I could have been trampled by a herd of our goats when I was four years old. Oh, yeah. I *was* trampled by a herd of goats.

Katie
Durham, North Carolina

6

Exotic Pets

When I was ten years old, my cat was hit by a car. To help mend my broken heart, my father got me a Silvertip Woolly monkey named Sheba. Now, I understand going from cat to monkey might seem drastic, but for a kid looking for a new furry companion, it was perfectly normal to me.

Some might think that Sheba was swinging from chandeliers, but that just wasn't the case. She was always a lady—well behaved and sensitive. Every night, I would dress Sheba in her PJs and put her to bed. We would cuddle and she would always tuck her furry little head just under my chin. Whenever I would bike to a friend's house, Sheba would sit on the handlebars, wrap her tail around my arm for balance, and off we would go. When I was old enough to drive, she would put on her seat belt and ride with me to go shopping. Whenever we went out, I would dress her in different outfits (not surprisingly, banana yellow was her favorite color). We were so inseparable back then that when I found the man of my dreams, I told him, "Marry me, marry my monkey." Fortunately, he fell in love with both of us.

Naomi
Acworth, Georgia

DEF LEOPARD

They couldn't understand why their cat went through so many scratchpads.

INTO THE WOODS

When Peter's buddy bailed on the camping trip, he decided to make the best of it.

THEY'VE GOT THE LOOK

Iguanas and turtlenecks sold separately.

TALES FROM A VET: HERE KITTY, KITTY

I've been a veterinarian for almost fifteen years and I'm often asked if I ever get bored with my job. How could I, when almost *every day* brings a new surprise? Which brings to mind Mrs. Ruth McDonald.

Ruth's husband had passed away, and so she became attached to her only child— her cat, Edna. After Edna passed, Ruth was grief-stricken. Her eyesight had deteriorated and I was worried about her being all alone. So, I was very excited when I looked at my schedule one morning and saw that Ruth was bringing in a new cat named Sasha. When Ruth came into my office holding her cat carrier, she was in great spirits. I asked her how she found her new companion. She told me that after Edna passed, she started feeding the neighborhood stray cats. Word apparently travels fast in the stray-cat community and soon she had many feline friends paying her visits. Ruth said that one cat in particular caught her attention because she only came by at night and for some reason, the other cats wouldn't socialize with her. Ruth felt sorry that this cat had no friends, so she would sit on the porch at night and wait for her. Eventually, a bond was formed and Ruth decided to keep her.

I peered into the carrier, and I cautiously pulled out the blanket with the warm little body wrapped inside, uncovering a precious little creature. And this is why my job is never dull: It turns out that the "cat" was not a cat after all, but rather a very large and hearty opossum. Opossums hiss like cats and happen to love cat food, so I understood the confusion. I looked up at Ruth, who was grinning from ear to ear as she said to me proudly, "Isn't she the most beautiful cat you've ever seen?" I paused for a moment and said, "Yes, she is." I guess love truly is blind.

REPTILES ON A FAMILY

Cats and dogs aren't the only kid-friendly pets.

ALL HAIL THE QUEEN

Beatrice often wondered what it would feel like to be a common gerbil.

AWKWARD GUINEA PIG NAME

Mii Mii Wii Wii

WEARING YOUR MARSUPIAL ON YOUR SLEEVE

This couple met while walking their sugar gliders.

RIBBIT

Their mother tried not to be offended when they thanked the toad first.

CLASSMATES

We all want to stand out in our school photo, and there's no better way than posing with our favorite pocket pals.

Jeremy
'92

PUMP UP THE VOLUME

Hair by opossum.

MONKEY BUSINESS

Unlike our children, there's no way to tell these Curious Georges to quit monkeying around.

WHITE HEAT

Just because they're naked doesn't mean we have
to be too.

ARM CANDY

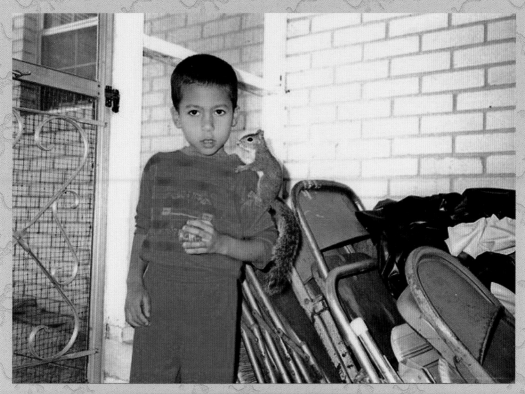

Joey didn't do anything without asking the squirrel first.

MY LITTLE SKUNK

"A pony isn't looking so crazy anymore, is it, Mom?"

BIG

Be careful what you wish for.

BEHIND THE AWKWARDNESS

This was my brother and me in a crib that our dad had built. Sitting with us— Sadie the cougar. We were supposed to be modeling my father's furniture, but who knows whether or not this confusing pic gave credit to his woodworking skills.

Corrina
Seattle, Washington

Just another photo where our parents forced us to dress up and look "nice" holding our pet rats so they could send it to our relatives to fawn over . . . is that not normal?

Elise
Dartmouth, Nova Scotia, Canada

This is a photo of my ferret and me when I was three. My aunt decided to surprise my parents and take me to the local PetSmart for a photo shoot. A toddler in suspenders, holding a parasol, with a pet ferret on her lap makes for one unforgettable photo.

Jackie
Griffith, Indiana

7

Holidays with the Pets

Our pets are good sports all year round, but there are times when their patience is truly tested, especially over the holidays. While they may not share all of our spirit, that doesn't stop us from wanting them to take part in our time-honored human traditions. So, we confuse them by dragging them to the mall to take photos with giant freakish bunnies and strange bearded men, cover them up in stars and stripes, and in the most perplexing move of all, we dress like them and walk around the neighborhood begging for food. So, while our idea of a celebration might include the exchanging of gifts, eating candy treats, and shooting off fireworks, for our pets the only part of the holidays worth celebrating is the fact that the family is all together.

BUNNY GOT YOUR TONGUE

Eight lives to go.

THE PATRIOTS

Let there be no doubt to whom these Chinese pugs pledge their allegiance.

SPOTTY

The dogs have decided to return to therapy.

SANTA'S LITTLE HELPER

You never know what you're going to get for Christmas.

JOLLY SAINT WHO?

They have no idea who Santa is, but that doesn't stop us from wanting our pets to meet him. Of course, all they care about is whether the fat guy will share his milk and cookies.

OH, CHRISTMAS STICK

While the birds liked their stick, they couldn't help but notice the *tree*.

SNUFFLEUPAGUS

For the horse, the costume felt redundant.

RED ROOSTER

She wanted to be sure she would wake up early on Christmas morning.

Floyd decided to get an early start on his midlife crisis.

PARTY LIKE IT'S YOUR BIRTHDAY

While it may be a milestone worth celebrating for humans, our pets are just wondering when they can take the hats off.

Hey, 10 Year-Old!

HOP FINN

This Easter Bunny was tired of sharing the spotlight with the eggs.

'TIS THE SEASON

Shortly after taking this photo, the dog converted.

HOLIDAY CHEER

It's the most wonderful time of the year
. . . for us.

147

That was the moment they vowed to never chase a bunny again.

MERRY KISSMAS

Mistletoe doesn't just apply to humans.

BEHIND THE AWKWARDNESS

This is Teddy Ratsevelt, a very friendly rat who loved to go outside on our shoulders. I managed to find him a turkey costume (thank you, Internet!) and my daughter took him trick-or-treating. We had to throw in some M&M's to keep him happy.

Nancy
Hyde Park, NY

I had this idea that dressing up my Flemish giant rabbit, Little Buddy, in a Christmas outfit would be a sweet card. Buddy was not happy, and let's just say the costume didn't survive the photo shoot.

Dharma
Reno, Nevada

First, my mom made my
brother and me pose together
as Joseph and Mary, which
was weird for us for obvious
reasons. And then Daisy
decided to eat Baby Jesus.

Brittany
Escondido, California

This is a photo of me (in
the front) and my sister
about ten years ago.
We were competitive
horseback riders back
then, and my mom
seriously wanted this
for our Christmas cards.
Look at the horse's face
. . . even she knew it
was lame.

Carlee
Munhall, Pennsylvania

8

Awkward Pets

There is no doubt we provide plenty of cringeworthy moments, but after looking through all of our submissions, we realized that every now and then our pets do something that makes *us* feel uncomfortable. Whether it's the excessive licking, the PDA, or the strange positions, they too have a penchant for odd behavior. It's at these times that we're reminded that nobody is immune to awkwardness.

CAUGHT IN THE ACT

Nibbles is still waiting for the proof.

NIGHTCAP

Amelie also makes a great pair of mittens.

Bates hasn't been getting much sleep lately.

BUM SNIFFER

One of the early signs of crack addiction.

CALL OF THE WILD

Some animal instincts can't be controlled.

Show-off.

JUNKSHOW

Kelly was prepared to do whatever she had to do to get their attention.

PLAYED-OUT

"Don't toy with me."

HERE'S LICKING AT YOU, KID

Their love will not be denied.

BEHIND THE AWKWARDNESS

We are sure Bennie grows thumbs when we leave him. He has separation anxiety and he hates being left alone, so one day he managed to push open a window on the second floor and scale up to the peak of the third floor. We thought we had a weathervane.

Cathie
Olney, Maryland

A photo of my cat, Tofu. She doesn't like cold weather much. In winter, after we cook dinner, she sometimes curls up in the frying pan because of the warmth.

Natasha
Kaohsiung, Taiwan

This is a photo of me and my parents' first dog, Snoopy, who had a talent for grabbing people's attention. At that age, I couldn't compete.

Darcy
Pewaukee, Wisconsin

Conclusion

I t's safe to say that our pets could probably do without our overindulgences, but if we were to just act normal, would they really be any happier? Conveniently for us, they don't speak human but here's what we think they would say:

Yes, it's a little uncomfortable when you make us wear sweaters, scarves, dresses, capes, necklaces, and reindeer antlers. Sure, birthdays and holidays are important celebrations for you, but for us, they only mean one thing—LOUD NOISES!!! Doesn't feel so good, does it? And we hate to break it to you, but we think your obsession with wanting to take photos of us is odd (FYI, it's really confusing when you tell us to smile even though we're already smiling).

We might never understand some of the things you do—correction, most of the things you do—but we know that they come from the right place and that while every awkward gesture may cause a little cringe, they also bring a lot of love.

Sincerely,
Your Pets

We couldn't have said it better ourselves.

Guest Contributors

KAREN McCULLAH: She is a screenwriter and novelist. Her film credits include *10 Things I Hate About You, Legally Blonde, She's the Man, The Housebunny,* and *The Ugly Truth*. Her novel *The Bachelorette Party* will coming to the screen soon. Sadly, Millie passed away and Karen is now eagerly awaiting her reincarnation.

KAREN NICHOLS: Karen Nichols is a cat writer/artist in the San Francisco Bay Area and a member of the Cat Writers Association. She is the creator of *The Cat's Meow Blog* (CatsMeowBlog.com) on Catster, and is the managing editor of *mousebreath!* (mousebreath.com), an online lifestyle magazine for cats. Currently, Karen is finishing work on the book *Man Up Your Cat in 30 Days*. She and her husband, Jeff, have three awkward family cat photo subjects: Skeezix, Mao, and Trip.

JENNIFER JOHNSON: Jennifer Johnson lives in a small town in Minnesota you've never heard of. She left a cushy job in the financial industry prior to its epic demise and is now the proud semi-super mom to Blake and Molly. (The best kids ever.) She sends a special shout-out to her hubby, Nick, who keeps her feet on the ground and when necessary, her meds organized. Current owner of a formerly obese housecat, Blazer.

ERICA WESSELER: Erica Wesseler is currently studying to be a high school math teacher. Her family has grown since this photo, not in goats but with in-laws, a new nephew, and a dog named Boysie. In true Wesseler fashion, her most recent family photo as well as her senior pictures included Boysie as well.

NAOMI SHEDD: Naomi is a motivational speaker, author, counselor, and teacher. She has been married to Tim for the past twenty-eight years. They have three adult children, and a blue-eyed charmer of a Rag doll cat, who they have never officially named. Naomi writes a blog called *Professional Parenting* (professionalparenting.wordpress.com). She has authored *Pictures with a Purpose* to help others learn how to use their scrapbooks to document and pass down their heritage of faith and is currently working on her second book, *Parenting On Purpose*.

Photo Contributors

Page 10: Tyler & Amy Harper; Page 12: The Hunt Family; Page 13: Ernie Smith; Page 14: Ken Priest, photographer; Page 15: Mr. & Mrs. Scallop Holden & "Bones"; Page 16: The Huffman Family (top), Naomi Shedd (right middle), Julie Host-Vanderheyden (right bottom), Brooke Mallory, photographer, and Sage Mallory, model (left); Page 17: animalphotography.com; Page 18: Karina Meerman; Page 19: Benjamin & Nettie Beck; Page 20: Anonymous (top), Kristin Johnson and Deborah Hildebrand (right middle), Alex, Julie & Lauren Bauwens (bottom right), The Atkins Family (left); Page 21: Stacy; Page 22: Kelsey, Ansel, Bo & Shishy; Page 23: Lisa Germant (top), Vicki Parker (left middle), Eryka Blank (left lower), Tonya Battistoni (right); Page 24: Betsy & Tim Mahoney; Page 25: The Finlayson Family; Page 26: Brennon & Captain Poynor/Thomas M. Green photographer; Page 27: The Hyde Family; Page 28: Kim & Angie C; Page 29: The Smith Family; Page 30: Becky L; Page 31: Grainger Cousins of Dog Pound; Page 32: Karen McCullah; Page 34: Anonymous; Page 35: Photo taken by Tami Anderson; Page 36: E. J. Wilson & Celeste; Page 37: Vijay & Stephanie D'Souza; Page 38: Lindsay & Erik Manly (top), Anonymous (right), Kristen Wallevand (left); Page 39: Billy Shepherd; Page 40: Chelsea Ward; Page 41: The O'Brochta Family; Page 42: Hannah Farwell; Page 43: Nicole & Kristine Carey (top), The Halberstadt Family (left middle), The Lightfoot Family (lower left), The Passut Family (right); Page 44: Kbillz; Page 46: Jeffrey & Melissa Mowery; Page 47: Jeffrey & Melissa Mowery; Page 48: Jackie Waldman & Snuffy; Page 49: Tara Renk Turner; Page 50: Anonymous; Page 51: Taylor; Page 52: Top: Esmond & Adam (top), Randen Erickson (right), Laura & Matt Starnes (left); Page 53: Jill Aiko Yee; Page 54: Luis Ramirez; Page 55: Sam & Kate Schilling; Page 57: Joshua from San Francisco; Page 58: India Bowen; Page 59: Jeff Simmons; Page 60: Rick O'Leary & Kelly Lazlo (top), The Galka Family (bottom); Page 61: Jillayne M. Tompkins; Page 62: Karen Nichols; Page 64: Vicki Warrenfells Rickabaugh; Page 65: The Klijian Family; Page 66: Mary Stewart; Page 67: Emily Giroux & Leah Thompson; Page 68: Mr. Gray (top), Anonymous (right), Tim Madden (left); Page 69: Nick & Jake Schleicher; Page 70: Vanessa Barneveld; Page 71: The Jones Family; Page 72: Alex (top), Terry & Urbano Piña (bottom); Page 73: Jake; Page 74: Gillian; Page 76: Stefanie & Courtney; Page 77: The Freese Family; Page 79: Anonymous; Page 80: Anonymous; Page 81: Zoe Nieman (top), Daniela Wasilewski (left), Tiffany Arnold Quintana (right); Page 82: Jennifer Nicole Johnson; Page 84: Jacob Schwarz; Page 85: Anonymous; Page 86: Ridge Sampels; Page 87: Aliza L. Wilson (top), Isabel Craig (right), Anonymous (left); Page 88: Anne Achneidervin; Page 89: Shannon & Julianna Welch; Page 90: Jennifer Cody; Page 91: Kathy Farro (top), Loren (bottom); Page 92: Robin and Russell

Lyman (top), Matt Wing (right), Gary Angle (left); Page 93: Boldly Brynn Photography; Page 94: The Wesseler Family; Page 96: Stephanie; Page 97: Anonymous; Page 98: Eric & Sharon Hershey (top), Bree Krawl (right), Ben & Snowflake (left); Page 99: Tom Casey; Page 100: Stephens & Weisenbacher Gang; Page 101: The Morrow Family; Page 102: The Bradley Family; Page 103: Lisa Girard; Page 104: The Kinions; Page 105: Soquel (left), The Rexford Family (right), Ari Glogower (bottom); Page 106: Paige & Lynn (top); The Izatt Family (bottom); Page 107: Katie Smith; Page 108: Naomi Shedd; Page 110: Stepahnie & Bailey; Page 111: Abbie; Page 112: The Bartos Family; Page 114: The Shields Family (top), Deanna Frink & Veronica Rowe (right), Devan & Lindsey Parker (left); Page 115: Abby Zubkousky-Nelson & Stacy Zubkousky; Page 116: Anonymous; Page 118: The Huffman Family; Page 119: Dana & Shauna Huth; Page 120: Erin E. Smith (top), Roxanne Butter (right), Jeremy R. Weiss (left); Page 121: Jamie Teal & Aunt Lana; Page 122: Bill & Steve Miller (top), Natalie & Rick Alia (right center), Donna (Love) Bauer (right bottom), Anonymous (left); Page 123: Anonymous; Page 124: D. A. Brascott Photography; Page 125: Joseph East; Page 126: Leslie Jones; Page 127: The Cramer Family; Page 128: Dale Griffith (top), Snow-Kropla Family (bottom); Page 129: Jackie Lopez; Page 130: The Tualla Family; Page 132: Anonymous; Page 133: Kelly H, Harley, Dixie & Sophie; Page 134: Jackie & Sarah; Page 135: Naomi Shedd; Page 136: Acott Chambers (top), Jenny Robinson (middle), Aleena & Adair Spotswood (bottom right), Abby Walker and Mrs. & Santa (Jerry) Claus (left); Page 137: Janet & Her Gang; Page 138: Michael, Kathy, & Christina Petera; Page 139: Guyver, Skyler & Myca Hopkins; Page 140: Amy Palmer; Page 141: Marcy Hodel; Page 142: Denise (top), Natalie (right), Amanda Edwards (left); Page 143: Julie & Jana Turner; Page 144: The Kanner Brothers; Page 145: Stacie Stephens, Jake Morrison, Jessica Sorensen (photographer); Page 146: Tristen R. Croghan (top), Thomas Hofren (right), The Huffman Family (lower left), Brian & Beth Feola (upper left); Page 147: Tony Salvador; Page 148: Sally A. Miska; Page 149: Donna (Love) Bauer; Page 150: Anonymous (top), Dharma Klock (bottom); Page 151: Britany V (top), The Mercuri Family (bottom); Page 152: Bogie; Page 154: Sue; Page 155: Chris R. Robinson & Amelie; Page 156: H. Due; Page 157: Edie & Maude; Page 158: Anne Edwards (top), Carly Rae (middle right), Cynthia Foss (bottom), The Jones Knighton Family (middle left); Page 159: Keri & Keith Donald; Page 160: The Wilson Family; Page 161: Anonymous; Page 162: Peggy; Page 163: Cole & Kat Higbee; Page 164: The Garofalo & Lucas Family; Page 165: Natasha Hodel (top), Patrick Naugle (bottom); Page 166 (Collage): Mosley; Claire Hunt & Kelly Kahle; Jim, Rachel, Cindy Fitzpatrick & Jack; Katie Habert; Jennifer Rose; The Bahl Family; Linda Scholfield; Maya Moran & Molly; Karen Louey; Carl & Tracy Thomas-Beyer; Janet Lang; Rebecca Brown; Jane Baker & Collin McFadden; Shelby Norman; Ashly Russell; Cheri Morris; Danny Look; Howell Family; M. D. Welch; Crista by cathyt71.imagekind.com; Britany; The Simmons Family; Geret, Noreen & Jim Coates; Tracy Nudd; Laura; Cynthia Vanosdale; The Gonzales Family; Melly Lindsey; Lucky, Spooky & Krista Eady; Julianne Breaux Pulvirenti; Leyda Greenwood; The McIntyre Family; Casey; Villareal Girls; The Angersola Family; Rachel Maness; Michelle Mullin & Carol; Noelle Piercy; Jon & Hanna Edison; Oscar & Tony Salvador (photographer); Jenny Robinson; Dennis .L & Shevon S.; Amy Newman & Nick Heiert; The McDanel Family; Teri Rabenberg Vitus & Debi Rabenberg-Locke; Justin; Aaron & Mr. Whiskers; Melanie & Christina Dorsen; Grier Filley; Beth & John; Ken Priest; Sarah & Natalie Stibitz; Anastasia & Elliott; Stephen Kolb Gilliland; Amy Kaufman & Peter Ryan; Molly Haynes; The Spear Family; Kristen Stone; Jay & Norma Pecotte; Brian; Emily & Kelly Sherman; The Rezayazdi Family; Becky Morey & Alex Bucher; Margo & John Watson; Amber Fields & Magic; Raider the Grape; Patrick Byrd; The Campbell Family; Hilary Emerson Lay; Sarah O.; The Huffman Family; Meredith S.; Ryan Kinder Photo by Lea Pittman; Jen & Eric E.; Michael & Kyle Mroz; Millie; The Briffa Family; Kristin & Kelsey Taylor; Erin & Colleen Gendron; Leigh, Amanda & Kimmi Nelson; Liam James T. Muttagh; The Sunshines Family; The Walton Mills Family; Kate; Reitz Family; Matt & Tasa Robinson; Jill Probst; Ben & Padraic; The Marrow Family; Joshua Erickson; Helena Freeman; Tom Allen; Lindsey Parker; Kacie Cleary; Kelsey Schoenknecht; The Scott Family; Grace;Page 175: Julia Varga Photography—The Art of Life/juliavarga.com

Acknowledgments

WE WOULD LIKE TO THANK: All of the families who have so generously shared their awkward pet photos with us; the Awkward Team—Blaire Bercy and Joe Hoyle; our literary agent, Rebecca Oliver, whose invaluable guidance made it possible for two awkward guys to actually become published authors; Adrianna Alberghetti, Greg Hodes, and SuzAnn Brantner; our licensing agent and part-time Evel Kneivel Sky-Sicle model, Ken Abrams; our lawyers, Allison Binder, Rick Genow, Greg Beattie, Alain Lapter; Pat Dunn; Chris Bender, JC Spink, and Jake Weiner at Benderspink; David Thalberg and Marissa Hermo at Krupp; Warren Adelman, Gabe Williams, Todd Cluff, and Terri Helman at GoDaddy; our official AFP photographer, Julia Varga; Rebecca Howard at AOL/Huffington Post; friends of AFP Amy Hertz, Zoe Triska, Mish Whalen, Kwala Mandel, Dave Shaw, Clay Tweel, Eric Poses, Justice Laub and Jill Yee, Alan Ou, Jen Weiner, Judd Apatow, China Chow, Amanda Goldberg, Joel Stein, David Byrne, Adam Herz, Margaret Gregory, Julie Chang, Allie MacKay, Ashley Cheung, Jim Hasson, JennyAnn Wheeler, Josh Spector, Claudia Perrone, Jana Turner and everyone at the OK Store in Los Angeles; of course, we will always be grateful to Kevin Mulhern at 94 WHJY; the team at Three Rivers Press—Tina Pohlman, Campbell Wharton, Catherine Pollock (who can also be found on page 116), Jonathan Lazzara, Sarah Breivogel, Maria Elias, Elizabeth Rendfleisch, Luisa Francavilla, Rachelle Mandik, Anna Thompson, and Suzanne O'Neill, our editor and unofficial third author whom we thank for her unwavering support, enthusiasm, and for being the one person we know will always be excited to receive a photo of a dog in a desk drawer.

MIKE BENDER WOULD LIKE TO THANK: My incredibly supportive family—my parents, Jules and Rebecca Bender, for their inspiration and for always taking such good care of Din-Din when I'm away; SuChin Pak for her love, support, and sense of humor; Suhyun Pak, Chris and Kristi Bender, Emmy and Selma Bender, Kenny and Selma Furst—the "AFP Grandparents" and most amazing grandparents in the world; Aunt Simone, Larry Hirschenbaum, Uncle Rick, Andrew Towbin, Nicole Towbin, Daniel Towbin, Steve Elkind, Gabe Elkind, Uncle Jerry, Aunt Vivian, Martin and Jackie Bender, Andy Klampert; my friends Matt Bijur, Tim Loree, Alex Baydin, Shannon Reilly Fidyk, Ryan Kroft, Adam Zeller, Robert Rave, Diana Hong, Annie Yun, Russell, Bobbi, and Sara Burrows. Special thanks to Chata and the sister I never had, Karen Lutz, who so thoughtfully took the time to contribute to this book. Her dog, Millie, will be greatly missed. And finally, to Din, who teaches me something valuable every day, but mostly that uncomfortably long stares can in fact be comfortable.

DOUG CHERNACK WOULD LIKE TO THANK: My wife, Amy, for her love, support, and advice; my son, Ravi, who makes every day worthwhile; my parents and brother for their love and encouragement and for getting me my first pet so I would stop feeding the raccoons in our backyard; Leon, Rob, and Risa Weinstock; Larry, David, Stephanie, Kenny, Raysa, George, and Irene Brociner; Glen and Laura Estersohn; Phyllis and Steven Brociner; Barrie and Bob Blumenthal; Stephen Donowitz and Jill Blumenthal; Wayne Steinberg and Lisa Blumenthal; Grandma Ethel, Ruth, and Grammie, who I'm sure would get a kick out of this; Phyllis and Bill Powell; Kelly and Jared Solomon; Debbie, Brian, and Rachel Crum; Cynthia, Amy, Ryan, and Nicole Turncliff; Sherry, David, Maria, and David Shollenbarger; Matt Hinton, Alan Donnelly, Ben Padnos, Keith Richman; and of course my pet goldfish, Porky, for being my Zen master, for swimming to the top of the bowl when my son wants to see you, and most important, for being hairless and not triggering any of my allergies.

About the Authors

MIKE BENDER is a screenwriter whose credits include *Not Another Teen Movie* and the MTV Movie Awards. Mike's dog, Din-Din, had final approval over his author photo.

DOUG CHERNACK has created and produced television shows for E!, Fox Sports, and the Golf Channel. He has been known to take his fish, Porky, on walks around the block.